Rainforest Workout

Clare Hibbert

Published by Evans Brothers Limited
2A Portman Mansions
Chiltern Street
London W1U 6NR

Reprinted 2010

Produced for Evans Brothers Limited by
White-Thomson Publishing Ltd

Printed in China by Midas Printing International Ltd

Educational consultant: Sue Palmer MEd FRSA FEA
Project manager: Clare Hibbert
Picture research: Amy Sparks
Design: Balley Design Limited
Creative director: Simon Balley
Designer/Illustrator: Michelle Tilly

British Library Cataloguing in Publication Data

Hibbert, Clare, 1970–
Rainforest workout. - (Sparklers. Body moves) 1. Movement (Acting) - Juvenile
literature 2. Exercise - Juvenile literature 3. Role playing - Juvenile literature
4. Rain forests - Juvenile literature
I. Title II. Palmer, Sue
792'.028

ISBN: 978 0 2375 3436 3

Contents

In the rainforest

drip!

drip!

Rainforests are hot and rainy.

Are you ready to try out

some rainforest moves?

5

Falling rain

pitter

patter

Rain falls in the forest every day.

wriggle

Move your arms up and down
to show the pouring rain.

7

Tree frog

slimy skin

This little frog lives high in a tree.

Moving around

These children are going through the forest in a boat.

splish

splosh

How *fast* can you paddle?

Big Cat

stripy!

A tiger hunts with its body close to the ground.

How **quietly** can you **prowl?**

hold on tight!

Now pretend to climb like this baby gorilla!

How *fast* can you **move** when you are balancing?

Marching elephant

This elephant is lifting up a log.

Pretend you have a trunk.

19

Tall tree

Can YOU grow as tall as a rainforest tree?

tiptoes

Curl up to be the seed...
then stre-e-e-tch up high!

21

Sparklers books are designed to support and extend the learning of young children. The first four titles in the series won a Practical Pre-School Silver Award. The books' high-interest subjects link in to the Early Years curriculum and beyond. Find out more about Early Years and reading with children from the National Literacy Trust (www.literacytrust.org.uk).

Themed titles
Rainforest Workout is one of four *Body Moves* titles that explore the animals and climate of a geographic environment, while also stimulating physical activity and role play. The other titles are:
Desert Workout   *Polar Workout*   *Underwater Workout*

A CD to accompany the series (available from Evans Publishing Group tel 0207 487 0920 or email sales@evansbrothers.co.uk) provides atmospheric noises from each environment, as well as popular songs and tunes to tie in with dance and gymnastic moves.

Areas of learning
Each *Body Moves* title helps to support the following Foundation Stage areas of learning:
Personal, Social and Emotional Development
Communication, Language and Literacy
Mathematical Development
Knowledge and Understanding of the World
Physical Development
Creative Development
If you work with children and want to take a child-led approach to movement, check out JABADAO (www.jabadao.org), who provide training in Developmental Movement Play and supply resources.

Making the most of reading time
When reading with younger children, take time to explore the pictures together. Ask children to find, identify, count or describe different objects. Point out colours and textures. Allow quiet spaces in your reading so that children can ask questions or repeat your words. Try pausing mid-sentence so that children can predict the next word. This sort of participation develops early reading skills.

Follow the words with your finger as you read. The main text is in Infant Sassoon, a clear, friendly font designed for children learning to read and write. The labels and sound effects add fun and give the opportunity to distinguish between levels of communication. Where appropriate, labels, sound effects or main text may be presented phonically. Encourage children to imitate the sounds.

You can also extend children's learning by using the books as a springboard for discussion and further activities. There are a few suggestions on the facing page.

Pages 4–5: In the rainforest

Make a mural, with children's paintings of rainforest animals on top of a background collage. If you can, listen to rainforest sounds while you work. Can children mimic the animals – roll into a ball like an armadillo, flap their wings like a parrot, hover like a hummingbird or slither like a snake?

Pages 6–7: Falling rain

Extend children's vocabulary by encouraging them to demonstrate different kinds of rain, for example a gentle shower or a heavy downpour. They could sing the song "I hear thunder".

Pages 8–9: Tree frog

Lay a hoop on the ground to represent a pool, so children can frog-hop in and out. If you have one, children can use a springboard and see how much further it enables them to jump. The song "Um um went the little green frog!" ties in nicely to this activity.

Pages 10–11: Moving around

While pretending to paddle, the children could sing the song "Row, row, row the boat". Encourage children to act out other ways to get around the forest. They could beat a path with a stick, cross a wobbly rope bridge through the trees or fly over the forest in a plane (with arms outstretched).

Pages 12–13: Big cat

Extend the prowling tiger activity so that children work in pairs, with one as the tiger and one as the prey. The prey cannot run away unless it hears the tiger moving. Make the tiger prowl over a crackly paper surface. If the tiger reaches the prey without making a sound – it can pounce!

Pages 14–15: Giant ape

Ask children to compare ordinary crawling to knuckle-walking like a gorilla. Which is faster – and which feels strongest? Suggest that children beat their chests. How does that make them feel?

Pages 16–17: Cheeky monkeys

Monkey-themed songs include "Three little monkeys, hanging from a tree" and "I went to the animal fair". Try a monkey fruit-picking activity, too, based on a relay race. The racer makes pretend climbing actions, then tosses their 'fruit' (a beanbag) to a partner, who makes the next leg of the 'climb'.

Pages 18–19: Marching elephant

There are lots of great elephant songs. Try "Nellie the elephant" or "Colonel Hathi's song" from *The Jungle Book*. Add structure to children's marching by suggesting that they take turns leading and following. The leader can change direction when you call the instruction "Turn!".

Pages 20–21: Tall tree

Ask questions during the tree-growing activity to make children more aware of their bodies. Ask children to identify which part of their body uncurls first – shoulders, elbows, head – and to practise growing very slowly. Next time, ask them to make the same moves very fast.

Index

Picture acknowledgements:
Corbis: 6 (Boyd & Evans), 10 (Jay Dickman), 13 b/g (DLILLC), 16 (Wolfgang Kaehle), 18 (Enzo & Paolo Ragazzin); **Getty Images:** 12 (Minden Pictures), 14 (Minden Pictures), 15 (Minden Pictures); **iStockphoto:** 9 (Andreas Huber), 22-23/24; **Photolibrary:** cover (Flirt/Corbis), cover/2-3/10/20/22-23/24 (Pacific Stock), 4-5 (Berndt Fisher), 8 (Michael Fogden), 19 (David Courtenay); **Shutterstock:** 21 b/g (Glen Gaffney); **WT-Pix:** 20 (Steve White-Thomson).

All other photographs by **Simon Punter**.